Master Your Time:

Proven Strategies to Boost Productivity and Achieve Your Goals

Andrew Ward

Time is our most precious asset, and I've often felt the frustration of trying to juggle multiple responsibilities while still feeling like there's never enough of it. Through my own journey of trial and error, I've discovered that effective time management is about making intentional choices and focusing on what truly matters. "Master Your Time: Proven Strategies to Boost Productivity and Achieve Your Goals" is a collection of the practical techniques and habits that have helped me transform my approach to time management and productivity. Whether you're a student, a professional, or someone seeking to improve your personal life, I hope the insights in this book will inspire and empower you to take control of your time and achieve your goals. Let's embark on this journey together and make every moment count.

Andrew Ward

Table of Contents

1. Introduction: The Importance of Time Management
2. Understanding Time and Productivity
3. Setting SMART Goals
4. Prioritizing Tasks Effectively
5. Techniques for Better Time Management
6. Overcoming Procrastination
7. Tools and Apps to Boost Productivity
8. Creating a Balanced Schedule
9. The Role of Habits in Time Management
10. Conclusion: Your Path to Mastery

Chapter 1: Introduction: The Importance of Time Management

Time is the most valuable resource we have. Unlike money or possessions, time is finite and irreplaceable. Every day, we are given 24 hours to use as we see fit, and how we choose to spend this time determines the quality and success of our lives.

The Value of Time

Imagine you have a bank account that credits your account each morning with £86,400. However, this balance doesn't carry over from day to day. Every evening, the bank deletes whatever part of the balance you failed to use during the day. What would you do? You would spend every cent, of course!

Each of us has such a bank. Its name is Time. Every morning, it credits you with 86,400 seconds. Every night, it writes off as lost whatever time you have failed to use wisely. It carries no balance forward and allows no overdraft. Each day, a new account is opened for you. Each night, it burns the remains of the day. If you fail to use the day's deposits, the loss is yours.

Why Time Management Matters

Effective time management is essential for achieving personal and professional success. By mastering the art of managing your time, you can increase your productivity, reduce stress, and make more time for the activities and people you love. Here are some reasons why time management is crucial:

1. **Increases Productivity**: Good time management skills enable you to work smarter, not harder. By organizing your tasks and prioritizing your responsibilities, you can accomplish more in less time.
2. **Reduces Stress**: When you have control over your time, you feel less overwhelmed and more in control of your life. This can significantly reduce stress and anxiety.
3. **Enhances Decision Making**: With proper time management, you have more time to think through decisions, leading to better choices and outcomes.
4. **Improves Work-Life Balance**: Effective time management allows you to allocate time for work, leisure, and rest, ensuring a more balanced and fulfilling life.
5. **Achieves Goals**: By managing your time well, you can set and achieve personal and professional goals more efficiently.

The Challenge of Modern Life

In today's fast-paced world, distractions are everywhere. Social media, emails, phone calls, and constant notifications can make it challenging to stay focused and productive. Moreover, the pressure to multitask can lead to decreased efficiency and burnout.

However, by developing strong time management skills and adopting proven strategies, you can navigate these challenges and take control of your time. This book will provide you with the tools and techniques you need to boost your productivity and achieve your goals.

What to Expect in This Book

In the following chapters, we will explore various aspects of time management and productivity. You will learn how to set SMART goals, prioritize tasks, and overcome procrastination. We will also delve into practical techniques and tools that can help you make the most of your time.

By the end of this book, you will have a comprehensive understanding of how to manage your time effectively and create a balanced, productive life. Whether you are a student, a professional, or someone looking to improve your personal life, the strategies in this book will empower you to master your time and achieve your dreams.

Let's begin this journey together and unlock the full potential of your most valuable asset—time.

Chapter 2: Understanding Time and Productivity

Before diving into specific strategies for managing your time, it's important to understand the concepts of time and productivity. By grasping these fundamentals, you'll be better equipped to implement the techniques discussed later in this book.

The Nature of Time

Time is a constant, ever-moving entity. It's unique because it's one of the few resources that is equally distributed to everyone, yet it's also one of the most squandered. To effectively manage your time, it's essential to recognize its true nature:

1. **Finite Resource**: Unlike other resources, time is limited and once it's gone, it cannot be recovered.
2. **Immutable**: Time cannot be paused, sped up, or slowed down. It continues regardless of our actions.
3. **Equally Distributed**: Everyone gets the same 24 hours each day, making it a great equalizer in terms of potential productivity.

The Myth of Multitasking

Many people believe that multitasking is an efficient way to get more done in less time. However, research has shown that multitasking can actually reduce productivity and increase errors. Here's why:

1. **Cognitive Load**: Our brains can only focus on one task at a time. When we switch between tasks, our cognitive load increases, leading to mental fatigue.

2. **Quality of Work**: Multitasking often results in lower quality work because we are not giving our full attention to any one task.
3. **Time Loss**: Each time we switch tasks, our brains need time to adjust, which results in lost productivity.

The Power of Focus

Focus is the key to productivity. When you concentrate on one task at a time, you can complete it more efficiently and with higher quality. Here are some benefits of maintaining focus:

1. **Increased Efficiency**: Focusing on a single task allows you to complete it faster.
2. **Higher Quality**: Full attention to one task improves the quality of your work.
3. **Reduced Stress**: Concentration reduces the cognitive load and stress associated with juggling multiple tasks.

The Importance of Goals

Setting clear, achievable goals is crucial for effective time management. Goals provide direction and a sense of purpose, helping you stay focused and motivated. Here's how to set effective goals:

1. **SMART Goals**: Ensure your goals are Specific, Measurable, Achievable, Relevant, and Time-bound.
2. **Break Down Goals**: Divide larger goals into smaller, manageable tasks.
3. **Write Them Down**: Documenting your goals increases commitment and accountability.

Time Management Techniques

There are several time management techniques that can help you make the most of your time. Some of the most effective methods include:

1. **The Pomodoro Technique**: Work in focused intervals (usually 25 minutes) followed by a short break.
2. **Time Blocking**: Allocate specific time slots for different tasks or activities throughout your day.
3. **The Eisenhower Matrix**: Prioritize tasks based on their urgency and importance, categorizing them into four quadrants.

The Role of Energy Management

Time management is not just about managing your time; it's also about managing your energy. Here's why energy management is important:

1. **Peak Performance**: Aligning tasks with your energy levels can enhance productivity.
2. **Avoiding Burnout**: Balancing work with rest and rejuvenation prevents burnout and maintains long-term productivity.

Practical Steps to Boost Productivity

Step 1: Identify Your Peak Hours

Everyone has certain times of the day when they are most alert and productive. Identify your peak hours and schedule your most important tasks during these times.

Step 2: Minimize Distractions

Create an environment conducive to focus by minimizing distractions. This might include turning off notifications, creating a dedicated workspace, or using noise-canceling headphones.

Step 3: Practice Mindfulness

Mindfulness techniques, such as meditation or deep breathing exercises, can help you stay focused and reduce stress.

Step 4: Regular Breaks

Taking regular breaks is essential for maintaining productivity. Short breaks help to recharge your brain, leading to sustained focus and efficiency.

Conclusion

Understanding the fundamentals of time and productivity is the first step towards mastering time management. By recognizing the true nature of time, the fallacy of multitasking, and the power of focus, you can start implementing effective strategies to boost your productivity. Setting clear goals, managing your energy, and adopting practical time management techniques will pave the way for greater success and fulfillment in both your personal and professional life.

In the next chapter, we will delve deeper into setting SMART goals and how they can transform your approach to time management and productivity.

Chapter 3: Setting SMART Goals

Setting clear, achievable goals is the cornerstone of effective time management and productivity. Without well-defined goals, it's easy to drift aimlessly and waste valuable time. This chapter will delve into the importance of goal setting, introduce the SMART criteria, and provide a step-by-step guide to setting and achieving your goals.

The Importance of Goal Setting

Goals give you direction and a sense of purpose. They act as a roadmap, guiding you towards your desired outcomes. Here's why setting goals is crucial:

1. **Clarity and Focus**: Goals help you clarify what you want to achieve and focus your efforts on specific tasks.
2. **Motivation**: Having clear goals can motivate you to take action and persist through challenges.
3. **Measurement**: Goals provide a benchmark for measuring progress and success.
4. **Time Management**: Clear goals help you prioritize tasks and allocate your time effectively.

Understanding SMART Goals

SMART is an acronym that stands for Specific, Measurable, Achievable, Relevant, and Time-bound. This framework ensures that your goals are well-defined and attainable. Let's break down each component:

1. **Specific**: Your goal should be clear and specific. Vague or broad goals can lead to confusion and lack of direction. Ask yourself:
    - What exactly do I want to achieve?
    - Why is this goal important?
    - Who is involved?
    - Where is it located?
    - Which resources or limitations are involved?

    Example: Instead of saying, "I want to be healthy," specify, "I want to lose 10 pounds in three months by exercising and eating a balanced diet."

2. **Measurable**: Your goal should be measurable so you can track your progress and stay motivated. Consider the metrics you'll use to measure your success. Ask yourself:
    - How much?
    - How many?
    - How will I know when it is accomplished?

    Example: "I will track my weight loss progress by weighing myself every week."

3. **Achievable**: Your goal should be realistic and attainable. Setting overly ambitious goals can lead to frustration and demotivation. Ask yourself:
    - How can I accomplish this goal?
    - Do I have the necessary skills and resources?
    - What is the time frame?

    Example: "I will join a gym and hire a personal trainer to help me develop a workout routine."

4. **Relevant**: Your goal should align with your broader objectives and be relevant to your life. Ask yourself:
    - Is this goal worthwhile?
    - Is it the right time?
    - Does it align with my other goals?
    - Am I the right person to achieve this goal?

    Example: "Losing weight will improve my health and boost my confidence, which aligns with my long-term wellness goals."

5. **Time-bound**: Your goal should have a deadline to create a sense of urgency and prompt you to take action. Ask yourself:
    - When do I want to achieve this goal?
    - What can I do today?
    - What can I do six weeks from now?
    - What can I do six months from now?

    Example: "I will lose 10 pounds in three months."

Steps to Setting SMART Goals

1. **Brainstorm Your Goals**
    - Take some time to think about what you truly want to achieve.
    - Write down all your goals, big and small, without worrying about how realistic they are at this stage.
2. **Evaluate and Prioritize**
    - Review your list and evaluate each goal.
    - Prioritize your goals based on their importance and urgency.
3. **Define Your Goals Using SMART Criteria**

- Rewrite each goal to make it Specific, Measurable, Achievable, Relevant, and Time-bound.
- Ensure each goal is clear and detailed.

4. **Break Down Goals into Smaller Tasks**
    - Divide your goals into smaller, manageable tasks.
    - Create a step-by-step plan for achieving each goal.

5. **Set Deadlines**
    - Assign deadlines to each task and goal.
    - Use a calendar or planner to schedule your tasks and keep track of deadlines.

6. **Monitor Progress and Adjust as Needed**
    - Regularly review your progress towards your goals.
    - Adjust your plan and timelines as needed based on your progress and any new developments.

Example: Setting a SMART Goal

Let's walk through an example to illustrate how to set a SMART goal:

Initial Goal: "I want to improve my public speaking skills."

1. **Specific**: "I want to become a confident public speaker by joining a local Toastmasters club and delivering speeches."
2. **Measurable**: "I will deliver at least one speech per month and receive feedback from club members."
3. **Achievable**: "I will dedicate two hours per week to practice my speeches and participate in club meetings."
4. **Relevant**: "Improving my public speaking skills will enhance my career prospects and boost my confidence in professional settings."
5. **Time-bound**: "I aim to deliver my first speech within one month and become a competent speaker within six months."

Final SMART Goal: "I want to become a confident public speaker by joining a local Toastmasters club, delivering at least one speech per month, dedicating two hours per week to practice, and achieving competency within six months."

Tips for Staying on Track

1. **Visualize Success**: Imagine yourself achieving your goals and the positive impact it will have on your life.
2. **Stay Organized**: Use tools like planners, to-do lists, and digital apps to keep track of your tasks and deadlines.
3. **Celebrate Milestones**: Reward yourself for achieving milestones along the way to stay motivated.
4. **Seek Support**: Share your goals with friends, family, or a mentor who can offer support and encouragement.
5. **Stay Flexible**: Be prepared to adjust your goals and plans as needed based on your progress and any new circumstances.

Conclusion

Setting SMART goals is a powerful way to take control of your time and increase your productivity. By making your goals Specific, Measurable, Achievable, Relevant, and Time-bound, you can create a clear roadmap to success. Remember to break down your goals into smaller tasks, set deadlines, and regularly monitor your progress. With dedication and persistence, you can achieve your goals and unlock your full potential.

In the next chapter, we will explore effective strategies for prioritizing tasks, ensuring that you focus on the most important activities and make the best use of your time.

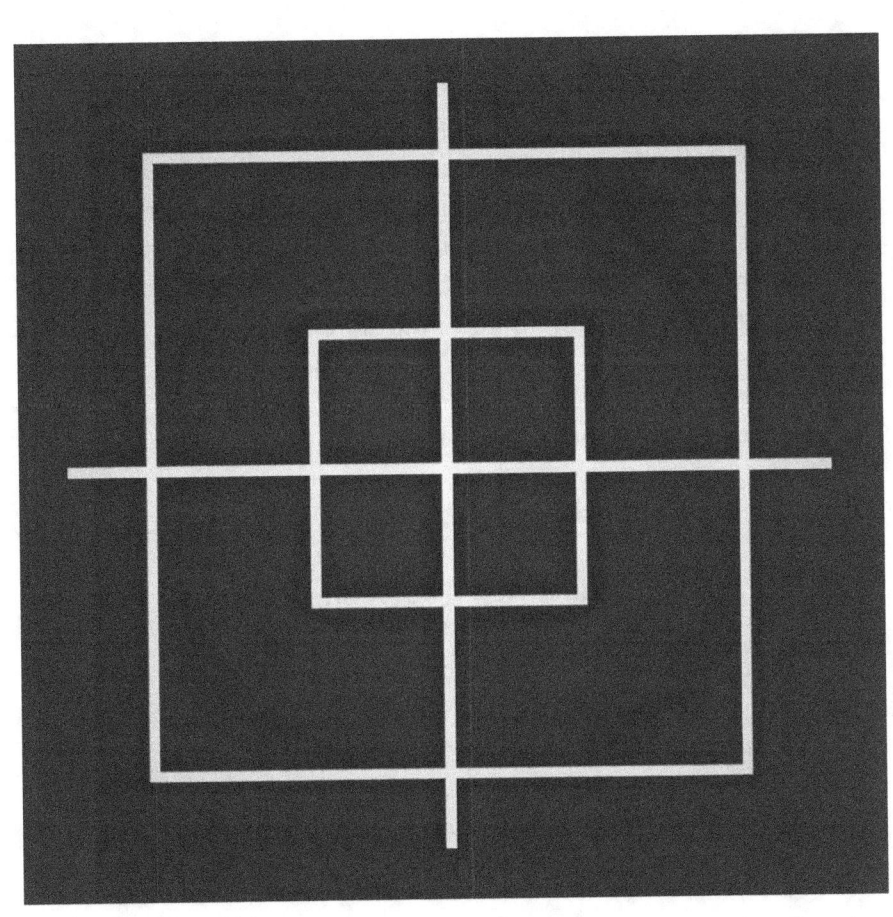

Chapter 4: Prioritizing Tasks Effectively

Prioritizing tasks effectively is crucial for managing your time and achieving your goals. With numerous responsibilities and distractions vying for your attention, it's essential to focus on the tasks that will have the most significant impact on your success. In this chapter, we will explore various prioritization techniques, tools, and strategies to help you identify and focus on what truly matters.

The Importance of Prioritization

Effective prioritization allows you to:

1. **Maximize Productivity**: Focus on tasks that offer the highest return on investment of your time.
2. **Reduce Stress**: By tackling high-priority tasks first, you prevent last-minute rushes and reduce stress.
3. **Achieve Goals**: Prioritization aligns your daily activities with your long-term goals.
4. **Improve Decision Making**: It helps in making informed decisions about where to invest your time and energy.

Techniques for Prioritizing Tasks

There are several proven techniques for prioritizing tasks. Here are some of the most effective ones:

1. **The Eisenhower Matrix**
    - **How It Works**: The Eisenhower Matrix, also known as the Urgent-Important Matrix, helps you categorize tasks into four quadrants:

- **Urgent and Important**: Tasks that require immediate attention and contribute to your goals. Do these first.
- **Important but Not Urgent**: Tasks that are crucial but can be scheduled for later. Plan these into your schedule.
- **Urgent but Not Important**: Tasks that need to be done quickly but do not significantly impact your goals. Delegate these if possible.
- **Not Urgent and Not Important**: Tasks that have little impact and can be postponed or eliminated. Avoid these tasks.

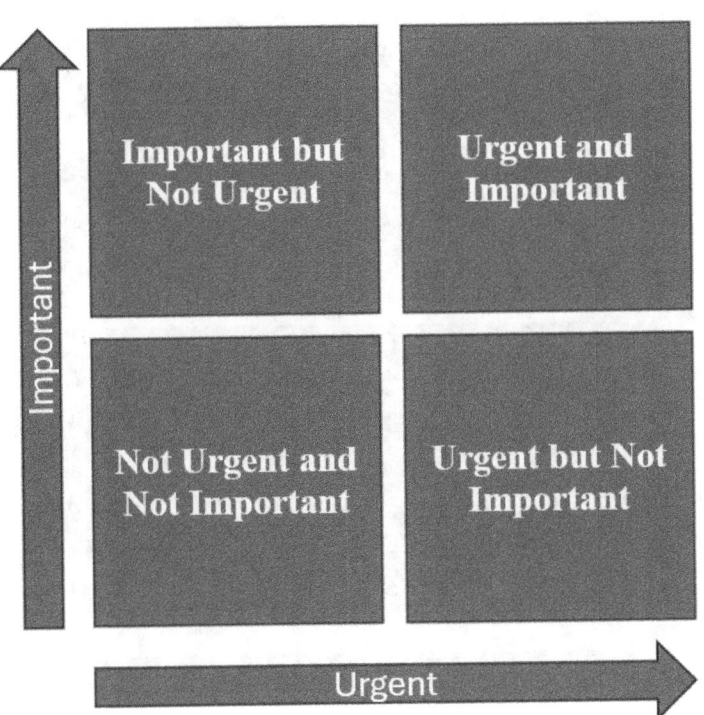

Example:

- **Urgent and Important**: Preparing for a major presentation due tomorrow.
- **Important but Not Urgent**: Working on a long-term project.
- **Urgent but Not Important**: Responding to non-critical emails.
- **Not Urgent and Not Important**: Browsing social media.

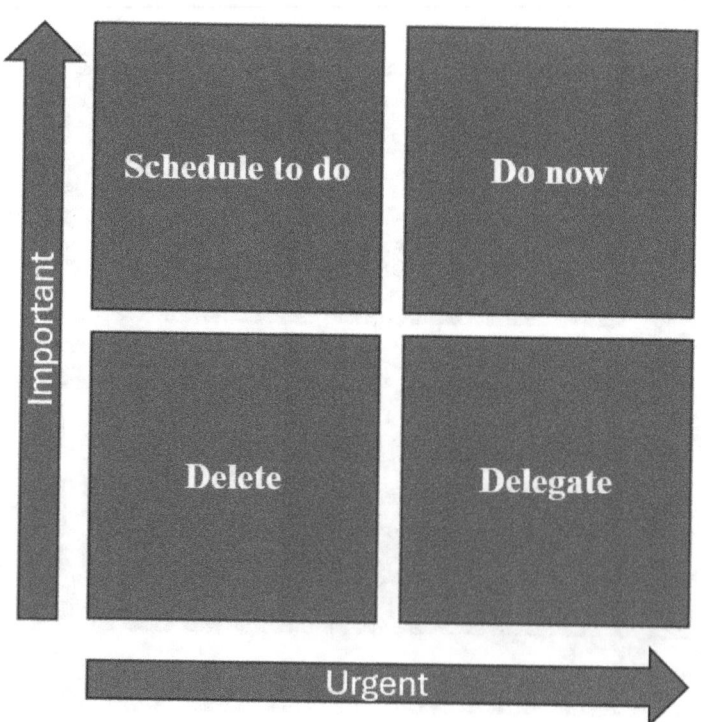

2. **ABCDE Method**
   - **How It Works**: The ABCDE method, popularized by Brian Tracy, involves categorizing tasks by priority:
     - **A**: Must-do tasks with serious consequences if not done.
     - **B**: Should-do tasks with mild consequences if not done.
     - **C**: Nice-to-do tasks with no consequences if not done.
     - **D**: Tasks to delegate.
     - **E**: Tasks to eliminate.
   - **Example**:
     - **A**: Completing a client project with a deadline today.
     - **B**: Attending a team meeting.
     - **C**: Organizing your desk.
     - **D**: Delegating routine admin tasks.
     - **E**: Deleting spam emails.

3. **Pareto Principle (80/20 Rule)**
   - **How It Works**: The Pareto Principle suggests that 80% of your results come from 20% of your efforts. Focus on the tasks that will yield the highest results.
   - **Example**: If you're a sales professional, focus on the 20% of clients that generate 80% of your revenue.

4. **MoSCoW Method**
    - **How It Works**: The MoSCoW method involves prioritizing tasks into four categories:
        - **Must Have**: Essential tasks that are critical to success.
        - **Should Have**: Important tasks that are not critical but add significant value.
        - **Could Have**: Desirable tasks that are not essential.
        - **Won't Have**: Tasks that can be deferred or eliminated.
    - **Example**:
        - **Must Have**: Fixing a major bug in software.
        - **Should Have**: Adding a new feature.
        - **Could Have**: Enhancing user interface design.
        - **Won't Have**: Minor tweaks that can wait for future updates.

Tools for Prioritization

Several tools can help you implement these prioritization techniques effectively:

1. **Digital Tools**
    - **Trello**: A visual tool for organizing tasks using boards and cards. You can create boards for each project and categorize tasks using labels and due dates.
    - **Asana**: A project management tool that allows you to create tasks, set priorities, and track progress.
    - **Todoist**: A task management app that lets you organize tasks, set priorities, and create recurring tasks.

2. **Physical Tools**
   - **Planner**: A physical planner can help you write down tasks and prioritize them using the techniques mentioned above.
   - **Bullet Journal**: A customizable journal system that allows you to track tasks, events, and goals.

Strategies for Effective Prioritization

1. **Identify Your Key Objectives**
   - Clearly define your short-term and long-term goals.
   - Align your daily tasks with these goals to ensure you are working towards what matters most.
2. **Break Down Large Tasks**
   - Divide larger tasks into smaller, manageable subtasks.
   - Prioritize these subtasks based on their impact and urgency.
3. **Set Realistic Deadlines**
   - Assign deadlines to your tasks to create a sense of urgency and focus.
   - Ensure that deadlines are realistic to avoid unnecessary stress.
4. **Review and Adjust Regularly**
   - Regularly review your task list and adjust priorities as needed.
   - Be flexible and willing to re-prioritize based on changing circumstances.
5. **Learn to Say No**
   - Protect your time by learning to say no to tasks and commitments that do not align with your goals or priorities.
   - Politely decline or delegate tasks that fall outside your critical priorities.

6. **Batch Similar Tasks**
    - Group similar tasks together and complete them in dedicated time blocks.
    - This reduces the cognitive load of switching between different types of tasks and increases efficiency.

Overcoming Common Prioritization Challenges

1. **Procrastination**
    - Break tasks into smaller steps and start with the easiest one to build momentum.
    - Use techniques like the Pomodoro Technique to work in focused intervals.
2. **Distractions**
    - Minimize distractions by creating a dedicated workspace, turning off notifications, and setting specific times for checking emails and messages.
3. **Overwhelming Task Lists**
    - Focus on the top three to five tasks each day that will have the most significant impact.
    - Delegate or eliminate tasks that are not essential.
4. **Balancing Multiple Projects**
    - Use a project management tool to track progress and deadlines for each project.
    - Prioritize tasks within each project based on their urgency and importance.

Case Study: Effective Prioritization in Action

Scenario: Sarah is a marketing manager juggling multiple projects and responsibilities. She often feels overwhelmed and struggles to meet deadlines.

Solution:

1. **Identify Key Objectives**: Sarah identifies her top goals: launching a new marketing campaign, completing a market research report, and mentoring a new team member.
2. **Break Down Tasks**: She breaks down each goal into smaller tasks. For the marketing campaign, tasks include developing a strategy, creating content, and scheduling social media posts.
3. **Use the Eisenhower Matrix**: Sarah categorizes her tasks:
   - **Urgent and Important**: Finalizing the campaign strategy.
   - **Important but Not Urgent**: Mentoring the new team member.
   - **Urgent but Not Important**: Responding to routine emails.
   - **Not Urgent and Not Important**: Planning the office party.
4. **Set Realistic Deadlines**: She sets deadlines for each task and blocks time in her calendar to work on high-priority items.
5. **Review and Adjust**: Sarah reviews her task list at the end of each day and adjusts priorities as needed.

Outcome: By implementing these prioritization strategies, Sarah feels more in control of her workload. She meets her deadlines, improves her productivity, and reduces stress.

Conclusion

Prioritizing tasks effectively is a vital skill for managing your time and achieving your goals. By using techniques such as the Eisenhower Matrix, ABCDE method, Pareto Principle, and

MoSCoW method, you can identify and focus on the tasks that matter most. Utilizing digital and physical tools can further enhance your ability to prioritize and stay organized. Remember to regularly review and adjust your priorities, learn to say no, and overcome common challenges to ensure you are consistently working towards your most important objectives.

In the next chapter, we will explore practical techniques for better time management, helping you make the most of every minute and boost your productivity.

Chapter 5: Techniques for Better Time Management

Effective time management is crucial for maximizing productivity and achieving your goals. In this chapter, we will explore a variety of practical techniques and strategies that can help you manage your time more efficiently. By implementing these techniques, you can take control of your schedule, reduce stress, and ensure that you are making the best use of your time.

The Pomodoro Technique

The Pomodoro Technique is a time management method developed by Francesco Cirillo in the late 1980s. It uses a timer to break work into intervals, traditionally 25 minutes in length, separated by short breaks. Here's how to implement it:

1. **Choose a Task**: Select a task you want to work on.
2. **Set a Timer**: Set a timer for 25 minutes (a "Pomodoro").
3. **Work on the Task**: Focus solely on the task until the timer rings.
4. **Take a Short Break**: Take a 5-minute break to recharge.
5. **Repeat**: After four Pomodoros, take a longer break (15-30 minutes).

Benefits:

- Enhances focus and concentration.
- Reduces mental fatigue.
- Encourages short breaks to maintain productivity.

Example: Let's say you need to write a report. You set your timer for 25 minutes and work solely on the report. After the timer rings, you take a 5-minute break to stretch or grab a coffee. Repeat this cycle four times, then take a longer break. This method keeps you focused and prevents burnout.

Time Blocking

Time blocking involves scheduling specific blocks of time for different tasks or activities. By dedicating time slots to particular tasks, you can ensure focused work periods without interruptions. Here's how to use time blocking effectively:

1. **Identify Tasks**: List all the tasks you need to complete.
2. **Allocate Time Slots**: Assign specific time blocks for each task or group of similar tasks.
3. **Stick to the Schedule**: Work on the assigned task during the allocated time slot without switching tasks.
4. **Review and Adjust**: At the end of the day, review your schedule and make necessary adjustments for the next day.

Benefits:

- Provides structure to your day.
- Reduces the likelihood of multitasking.
- Ensures dedicated time for important tasks.

Example: For instance, you might block out 9-11 AM for focused work on a major project, 11-12 PM for email and administrative tasks, 1-3 PM for meetings, and 3-5 PM for additional focused work or project follow-up.

The 2-Minute Rule

The 2-Minute Rule, popularized by productivity expert David Allen, states that if a task takes less than two minutes to complete, do it immediately. This simple rule can help you quickly clear small tasks from your to-do list and prevent them from piling up.

Steps:

1. **Identify Quick Tasks**: Review your to-do list and identify tasks that can be completed in less than two minutes.
2. **Complete Immediately**: Perform these tasks right away instead of postponing them.
3. **Focus on Larger Tasks**: Once the quick tasks are done, focus on more substantial tasks without distraction.

Benefits:

- Quickly reduces the number of small tasks.
- Prevents procrastination on minor tasks.
- Helps maintain momentum throughout the day.

Example: If you receive an email that requires a short response, a phone call to confirm an appointment, or a quick document review, handle these tasks immediately instead of adding them to your to-do list.

The Eisenhower Matrix

The Eisenhower Matrix, mentioned earlier in the book, is an effective prioritization tool that can also enhance your time management. By categorizing tasks based on urgency and importance, you can focus on what truly matters.

1. **Urgent and Important**: Do these tasks immediately.
2. **Important but Not Urgent**: Schedule these tasks for later.
3. **Urgent but Not Important**: Delegate these tasks if possible.
4. **Not Urgent and Not Important**: Eliminate or minimize these tasks.

Benefits:

- Helps prioritize tasks effectively.
- Reduces time spent on low-impact activities.
- Ensures focus on high-priority tasks.

Example: If you have an urgent report due today, it falls into the Urgent and Important category and should be tackled immediately. Planning next week's meeting agenda, which is Important but Not Urgent, can be scheduled for later in the week.

Batch Processing

Batch processing involves grouping similar tasks together and completing them in one focused session. This technique reduces the cognitive load of switching between different types of tasks and increases efficiency.

Steps:

1. **Identify Similar Tasks**: Group tasks that are similar in nature (e.g., answering emails, making phone calls).
2. **Schedule Batch Sessions**: Allocate specific time blocks for each batch of tasks.
3. **Work Continuously**: Focus on completing the tasks in each batch without interruption.

Benefits:

- Increases efficiency by reducing task-switching.
- Enhances focus on specific types of tasks.
- Helps manage time more effectively by organizing similar activities together.

Example: Set aside one hour each morning to process emails, one hour in the afternoon to make phone calls, and another dedicated block for administrative tasks.

The ABCDE Method

The ABCDE Method, also covered earlier, is a powerful prioritization technique that can streamline your time management efforts. Here's a recap of how to use it:

1. **Categorize Tasks**: Assign each task a letter from A to E based on its priority:
   - **A**: Must-do tasks with serious consequences if not done.
   - **B**: Should-do tasks with mild consequences if not done.
   - **C**: Nice-to-do tasks with no consequences if not done.
   - **D**: Tasks to delegate.
   - **E**: Tasks to eliminate.
2. **Focus on A Tasks**: Start with the most critical tasks (A) and work your way down the list.
3. **Delegate and Eliminate**: Delegate D tasks and eliminate E tasks to free up time for higher-priority activities.

Benefits:

- Clarifies task priorities.
- Ensures focus on the most impactful tasks.
- Simplifies decision-making about where to invest your time.

Example: An A task might be preparing for a critical client meeting, a B task could be updating a report that's due next week, a C task might be organizing your workspace, a D task could be delegating a routine data entry task, and an E task might be eliminating unnecessary meetings.

Mind Mapping

Mind mapping is a visual technique for organizing thoughts and tasks. It helps you brainstorm ideas, plan projects, and structure your tasks in a logical, interconnected manner.

Steps:

1. **Create a Central Idea**: Write the main task or project in the centre of a page or digital mind map tool.
2. **Add Branches**: Draw branches from the central idea, representing sub-tasks or related concepts.
3. **Add Details**: Add more branches and details as needed, breaking down each task into smaller components.
4. **Review and Organize**: Review the mind map and organize tasks based on priority and sequence.

Benefits:

- Provides a clear visual representation of tasks and projects.
- Enhances creativity and brainstorming.

- Helps identify connections and dependencies between tasks.

Example: If you're planning a product launch, start with the central idea "Product Launch." Branches might include "Marketing," "Production," "Sales," and "Customer Support." Under "Marketing," sub-branches could be "Social Media Campaign," "Email Marketing," and "Press Releases."

Time Management Apps and Tools

Using time management apps and tools can significantly enhance your ability to manage tasks and stay organized. Here are some popular options:

1. **Trello**: A visual tool for organizing tasks using boards, lists, and cards. Ideal for project management and collaboration.
2. **Asana**: A comprehensive project management tool that allows you to create tasks, set priorities, and track progress.
3. **Todoist**: A task management app that helps you organize tasks, set priorities, and create recurring tasks.
4. **RescueTime**: A time-tracking app that provides insights into how you spend your time and helps identify areas for improvement.
5. **Forest**: A productivity app that encourages focused work by growing a virtual tree during work sessions.

Benefits:

- Enhances organization and task management.
- Provides insights into time usage and productivity.
- Encourages accountability and focus.

Example: Using Trello, you can create a board for a specific project, add lists for each phase of the project, and create cards for individual tasks. Asana allows you to set deadlines, assign tasks to team members, and track progress visually. Todoist helps you prioritize daily tasks and set reminders for recurring activities. RescueTime runs in the background on your computer and mobile devices, tracking the time you spend on various applications and websites. Forest helps you stay focused by growing a virtual tree while you work, which dies if you leave the app prematurely.

Practical Steps to Implement Time Management Techniques

1. **Start Small**: Begin by implementing one or two techniques and gradually incorporate more as you become comfortable.
2. **Set Clear Goals**: Define your goals and prioritize tasks based on their alignment with these goals.
3. **Create a Schedule**: Use a planner or digital calendar to create a daily or weekly schedule, incorporating time management techniques.
4. **Review and Adjust**: Regularly review your progress and adjust your techniques and schedule as needed.
5. **Stay Consistent**: Consistency is key to effective time management. Stick to your chosen techniques and make them a habit.

Example: Start with the Pomodoro Technique to manage your daily tasks. Once you're comfortable, integrate time blocking to structure your day more efficiently. Set clear goals using the SMART criteria, and use the Eisenhower Matrix to prioritize your tasks. Create a weekly schedule that includes time blocks for different activities and review your progress at the end of each week. Stay consistent with these techniques, and gradually incorporate additional methods such as batch processing and the ABCDE Method.

Conclusion

Mastering time management requires a combination of effective techniques, practical tools, and consistent effort. By implementing strategies such as the Pomodoro Technique, time blocking, the 2-Minute Rule, the Eisenhower Matrix, batch processing, the ABCDE Method, and mind mapping, you can take control of your time and boost your productivity. Utilizing time management apps and tools can further enhance your ability to stay organized and focused. Remember to start small, set clear goals, create a schedule, review your progress, and stay consistent in your efforts. With dedication and practice, you can master your time and achieve your goals.

In the next chapter, we will explore how to overcome procrastination and develop habits that support effective time management and productivity.

Chapter 6: Overcoming Procrastination

Procrastination is one of the most common obstacles to effective time management and productivity. It's the act of delaying or postponing tasks, often leading to stress, missed deadlines, and decreased performance. In this chapter, we will explore the psychology behind procrastination, identify common triggers, and provide practical strategies to overcome it.

Understanding Procrastination

Procrastination isn't simply about poor time management; it's often a complex psychological behaviour driven by various factors. Understanding why we procrastinate is the first step toward overcoming it.

Psychological Factors:

1. **Fear of Failure**: The fear of not meeting expectations can lead to avoidance behaviours.
2. **Perfectionism**: Striving for perfection can paralyze you, making it difficult to start or finish tasks.
3. **Lack of Motivation**: Tasks that are perceived as boring or irrelevant can lead to procrastination.
4. **Overwhelm**: Feeling overwhelmed by the size or complexity of a task can result in delay.

Common Triggers:

1. **Task Aversion**: Dislike for the task at hand.
2. **Lack of Clear Goals**: Ambiguous or poorly defined tasks can make it hard to start.

3. **Immediate Gratification**: Preference for activities that provide instant pleasure over long-term benefits.
4. **Distractions**: Environmental factors, such as social media or noisy surroundings, can contribute to procrastination.

Strategies to Overcome Procrastination

Overcoming procrastination requires a combination of self-awareness, practical strategies, and sometimes, behavioural changes. Here are several effective methods:

1. **Break Tasks into Smaller Steps**

Large tasks can seem daunting and overwhelming, leading to procrastination. Breaking them down into smaller, manageable steps can make them feel more achievable.

Steps:

1. **Identify the Task**: Clearly define the task you need to complete.
2. **Divide into Subtasks**: Break the task down into smaller components.
3. **Set Milestones**: Establish mini-deadlines for each subtask.

Example: If you need to write a research paper, break it down into steps such as choosing a topic, conducting research, creating an outline, writing a draft, and editing.

2. **Use the 5-Minute Rule**

The 5-Minute Rule involves committing to work on a task for just five minutes. Often, starting is the hardest part, and once you begin, you're likely to continue beyond the initial five minutes.

Steps:

1. **Set a Timer**: Commit to working on a task for five minutes.
2. **Begin the Task**: Start working, knowing you only need to do it for a short time.
3. **Continue if Possible**: Once the timer goes off, assess if you can continue working.

Example: If you're procrastinating on cleaning your workspace, set a timer for five minutes. Once you start, you'll likely find it easier to keep going.

3. Prioritize Tasks with the Eisenhower Matrix

The Eisenhower Matrix helps prioritize tasks based on urgency and importance, enabling you to focus on what matters most and reduce procrastination.

Steps:

1. **Categorize Tasks**: Divide tasks into four quadrants: urgent and important, important but not urgent, urgent but not important, and not urgent or important.
2. **Focus on High-Priority Tasks**: Concentrate on tasks that are both urgent and important.
3. **Delegate or Eliminate Low-Priority Tasks**: Delegate urgent but not important tasks and eliminate those that are neither urgent nor important.

Example: If you have an urgent project deadline, prioritize it over less critical tasks like organizing files.

4. Implement Time Management Techniques

Techniques such as the Pomodoro Technique and time blocking can help you stay focused and make steady progress on tasks, reducing the tendency to procrastinate.

Steps:

1. **Pomodoro Technique**: Work in focused intervals (25 minutes) followed by short breaks.
2. **Time Blocking**: Schedule specific time blocks for different tasks and adhere to the schedule.

Example: Use the Pomodoro Technique to tackle a writing assignment. Work for 25 minutes, take a 5-minute break, and repeat.

5. **Create a Productive Environment**

Your environment can significantly impact your ability to focus and avoid procrastination. Create a workspace that minimizes distractions and fosters productivity.

Steps:

1. **Designate a Workspace**: Choose a quiet, dedicated area for work.
2. **Minimize Distractions**: Turn off notifications, use noise-cancelling headphones, and keep your workspace tidy.
3. **Use Productivity Tools**: Utilize tools and apps that block distracting websites or track your time.

Example: Set up a home office with minimal distractions and use apps like Freedom or StayFocusd to block social media during work hours.

6. **Set Clear and Achievable Goals**

Setting specific, measurable, achievable, relevant, and time-bound (SMART) goals can provide direction and motivation, reducing the likelihood of procrastination.

Steps:

1. **Define SMART Goals**: Make sure your goals are clear and attainable.
2. **Break Down Goals**: Divide larger goals into smaller, actionable steps.
3. **Track Progress**: Monitor your progress and adjust as needed.

Example: Instead of setting a vague goal like "get fit," set a SMART goal such as "exercise for 30 minutes three times a week for the next month."

7. **Use Accountability Partners**

Having someone to hold you accountable can provide motivation and encouragement, helping you stay on track and avoid procrastination.

Steps:

1. **Choose an Accountability Partner**: Select someone you trust who can help you stay accountable.
2. **Set Regular Check-Ins**: Schedule regular check-ins to discuss your progress and challenges.
3. **Provide Mutual Support**: Offer support and encouragement to each other.

Example: Partner with a colleague to share weekly progress updates and hold each other accountable for meeting deadlines.

8. **Reward Yourself**

Incentives can motivate you to complete tasks and reduce procrastination. Set up a reward system for completing tasks or reaching milestones.

Steps:

1. **Set Up Rewards**: Identify small rewards for completing tasks or achieving goals.
2. **Celebrate Milestones**: Recognize and celebrate your progress.
3. **Use Positive Reinforcement**: Use rewards to reinforce positive behaviour.

Example: Treat yourself to a favourite snack or a break to watch an episode of your favourite show after completing a challenging task.

9. **Address Underlying Issues**

Sometimes procrastination is a symptom of underlying issues such as anxiety, depression, or burnout. Addressing these issues can help reduce procrastination and improve overall well-being.

Steps:

1. **Identify Underlying Issues**: Reflect on whether stress, anxiety, or other factors are contributing to your procrastination.

2. **Seek Professional Help**: Consider speaking with a therapist or counsellor if needed.
3. **Practice Self-Care**: Engage in activities that promote mental and physical well-being, such as exercise, meditation, and adequate sleep.

Example: If you're feeling overwhelmed by a project, take a step back and assess whether you need to seek support or adjust your workload.

Practical Exercises to Overcome Procrastination

1. **Daily Reflection**:
   - Take a few minutes each evening to reflect on your day.
   - Identify tasks you procrastinated on and analyse why.
   - Plan strategies for the following day to address these challenges.
2. **Visualization**:
   - Visualize the successful completion of a task.
   - Imagine the positive outcomes and how you will feel once it's done.
   - Use this mental imagery to motivate yourself to start.
3. **Mindfulness and Meditation**:
   - Practice mindfulness to stay present and focused.
   - Use meditation techniques to reduce stress and anxiety, which can contribute to procrastination.
   - Incorporate short mindfulness exercises into your daily routine.
4. **Journaling**:
   - Keep a journal to track your thoughts and feelings about tasks.

- Write about your procrastination triggers and strategies to overcome them.
- Use journaling as a tool for self-reflection and growth.

5. **Time Audit**:
   - Conduct a time audit to understand how you spend your day.
   - Identify periods of procrastination and assess the reasons.
   - Use the insights to make adjustments and improve time management.

Conclusion

Overcoming procrastination requires self-awareness, practical strategies, and consistent effort. By understanding the psychological factors and common triggers, you can develop effective methods to tackle procrastination. Techniques such as breaking tasks into smaller steps, using the 5-Minute Rule, prioritizing with the Eisenhower Matrix, and creating a productive environment can significantly reduce procrastination. Setting clear goals, using accountability partners, rewarding yourself, and addressing underlying issues further enhance your ability to overcome procrastination and achieve your goals.

In the next chapter, we will delve into tools and apps that can help boost your productivity, providing practical solutions to streamline your workflow and manage your time more effectively.

Chapter 7: Tools and Apps to Boost Productivity

In today's digital age, there are countless tools and apps designed to enhance productivity and streamline workflows. Utilizing these resources can help you manage tasks more effectively, stay organized, and maintain focus. This chapter will explore a variety of productivity tools and apps, their features, and how they can be integrated into your daily routine to boost productivity.

Task Management and Organization Tools

1. **Todoist**

Todoist is a powerful task management app that helps you organize tasks, set priorities, and track progress.

Features:

- **Task Creation**: Easily create tasks and sub-tasks with due dates and priorities.
- **Projects and Labels**: Organize tasks into projects and categorize them with labels.
- **Recurring Tasks**: Set recurring tasks for regular activities.
- **Collaboration**: Share projects and tasks with team members for collaborative work.

How to Use:

- **Daily Planning**: Use Todoist to plan your daily tasks, prioritizing them based on importance and deadlines.
- **Project Management**: Organize large projects into smaller, manageable tasks and track progress.

Example: Create a project for a marketing campaign and add tasks such as "Develop strategy," "Create content," and "Schedule posts." Set deadlines and assign tasks to team members.

2. **Trello**

Trello is a visual project management tool that uses boards, lists, and cards to organize tasks and workflows.

Features:

- **Boards and Lists**: Create boards for different projects and lists for various stages of tasks.
- **Cards**: Add cards for individual tasks, including descriptions, due dates, and attachments.
- **Labels and Checklists**: Use labels to categorize tasks and checklists to track progress.
- **Collaboration**: Invite team members to boards for collaborative work.

How to Use:

- **Kanban Method**: Implement the Kanban method by creating lists such as "To Do," "In Progress," and "Done."
- **Workflow Management**: Use Trello to visualize workflows and move tasks through different stages.

Example: For a product launch, create a board with lists for "Planning," "Development," "Marketing," and "Launch." Add cards for tasks under each list and move them as they progress.

3. **Asana**

Asana is a comprehensive project management tool that helps teams plan, organize, and track work.

Features:

- **Task Assignment**: Assign tasks to team members with due dates and priority levels.
- **Project Timelines**: Visualize project timelines and dependencies with Gantt charts.
- **Task Comments**: Communicate directly within tasks through comments and updates.
- **Integrations**: Integrate with other tools such as Slack, Google Drive, and Outlook.

How to Use:

- **Project Planning**: Plan projects by creating tasks, setting deadlines, and assigning responsibilities.
- **Team Collaboration**: Use Asana to facilitate communication and ensure everyone is on the same page.

Example: For a website redesign, create a project with tasks like "Design mock-ups," "Develop front-end," and "Test functionality." Assign tasks to team members and track progress.

Time Management and Focus Tools

1. **RescueTime**

RescueTime is a time-tracking app that provides insights into how you spend your time on digital devices.

Features:

- **Activity Tracking**: Automatically track time spent on applications and websites.
- **Productivity Reports**: Receive detailed reports on your productivity and time usage.
- **Goal Setting**: Set goals for specific activities and track progress.
- **Focus Time**: Block distracting websites to maintain focus.

How to Use:

- **Time Audit**: Conduct a time audit to understand where your time is going and identify areas for improvement.
- **Goal Setting**: Set daily or weekly goals to limit time spent on distractions and increase productive time.

Example: Set a goal to spend no more than 30 minutes on social media per day. Use the reports to track your progress and adjust as needed.

2. **Forest**

Forest is a unique productivity app that helps you stay focused by growing virtual trees while you work.

Features:

- **Focus Sessions**: Set a timer for focus sessions, during which a virtual tree grows.
- **Tree Growth**: If you leave the app before the session ends, the tree dies.
- **Progress Tracking**: Track your focus time and build a virtual forest.

- **Collaboration**: Compete with friends to grow the largest forest.

How to Use:

- **Focus Blocks**: Use Forest to create focus blocks for uninterrupted work.
- **Gamification**: Motivate yourself by growing trees and building a virtual forest.

Example: Set a 30-minute timer to focus on writing a report. As you work, a tree grows in the app, and your virtual forest expands with each session.

3. **Pomodone**

Pomodone integrates the Pomodoro Technique with your existing task management tools to help you stay focused and productive.

Features:

- **Pomodoro Timer**: Use the built-in Pomodoro timer to work in focused intervals.
- **Task Integration**: Integrate with tools like Trello, Asana, and Todoist to sync tasks.
- **Time Tracking**: Track the time spent on each task and analyse productivity.
- **Break Management**: Schedule regular breaks to maintain focus and prevent burnout.

How to Use:

- **Task Syncing**: Sync your tasks from Trello or Asana and use the Pomodoro timer to work on them.

- **Time Analysis**: Review time-tracking reports to identify productivity patterns.

Example: Sync your Trello board with Pomodone, start a Pomodoro timer for a task, and work in 25-minute intervals with 5-minute breaks.

Note-Taking and Knowledge Management Tools

1. **Evernote**

Evernote is a versatile note-taking app that helps you capture and organize information.

Features:

- **Notes and Notebooks**: Create notes and organize them into notebooks.
- **Tags**: Use tags to categorize and easily find notes.
- **Web Clipping**: Clip web pages and save them directly to Evernote.
- **Integration**: Integrate with tools like Google Drive, Slack, and Outlook.

How to Use:

- **Meeting Notes**: Use Evernote to take notes during meetings and organize them by project or topic.
- **Research**: Clip articles and research materials from the web and save them in Evernote.

Example: Create a notebook for a project and add notes for meeting minutes, research, and ideas. Use tags to categorize and quickly find relevant information.

2. **Notion**

Notion is an all-in-one workspace that combines note-taking, task management, and collaboration.

Features:

- **Notes and Databases**: Create notes, databases, and tables.
- **Templates**: Use templates for project management, to-do lists, and more.
- **Collaboration**: Share pages and collaborate with team members in real-time.
- **Customization**: Customize the workspace to suit your needs.

How to Use:

- **Project Management**: Use Notion to create a project dashboard with tasks, notes, and timelines.
- **Knowledge Base**: Build a knowledge base for storing and organizing information.

Example: Create a project dashboard with sections for tasks, meeting notes, and resources. Use the Kanban board template to track task progress.

3. **OneNote**

OneNote is a digital note-taking app that integrates seamlessly with Microsoft Office.

Features:

- **Notebooks and Sections**: Organize notes into notebooks and sections.
- **Drawing Tools**: Use drawing tools to sketch ideas and annotate notes.
- **Audio Recording**: Record audio notes directly within the app.
- **Integration**: Integrate with Microsoft Office applications.

How to Use:

- **Class Notes**: Use OneNote to take and organize notes for different classes or subjects.
- **Brainstorming**: Sketch ideas and create mind maps using the drawing tools.

Example: Create a notebook for a marketing campaign with sections for brainstorming, meeting notes, and task lists. Record audio notes during brainstorming sessions for later reference.

Communication and Collaboration Tools

1. **Slack**

Slack is a messaging app designed for team communication and collaboration.

Features:

- **Channels**: Create channels for different projects, teams, or topics.
- **Direct Messaging**: Send direct messages to team members.

- **File Sharing**: Share files and documents within channels and messages.
- **Integrations**: Integrate with tools like Google Drive, Trello, and Zoom.

How to Use:

- **Team Communication**: Use channels to organize team communication by project or topic.
- **Collaboration**: Share files and collaborate on tasks within Slack.

Example: Create a channel for a product launch team to discuss updates, share files, and coordinate tasks. Use integrations to connect Trello boards and Google Drive documents.

2. **Microsoft Teams**

Microsoft Teams is a collaboration platform that combines chat, video meetings, and file storage.

Features:

- **Channels and Teams**: Create teams and channels for different projects or departments.
- **Video Meetings**: Host video meetings and share screens.
- **File Collaboration**: Collaborate on files directly within Teams.
- **Integrations**: Integrate with Microsoft Office and other productivity tools.

How to Use:

- **Project Collaboration**: Create a team for a project and use channels to organize communication.
- **Meetings and Calls**: Schedule and host video meetings with team members.

Example: Set up a team for a sales department with channels for different regions. Use video meetings for weekly check-ins and collaborate on sales reports in real-time.

3. **Zoom**

Zoom is a video conferencing tool that supports online meetings, webinars, and collaboration.

Features:

- **HD Video and Audio**: Host high-quality video and audio meetings.
- **Screen Sharing**: Share your screen or specific applications during meetings.
- **Breakout Rooms**: Create breakout rooms for smaller group discussions.
- **Recording**: Record meetings for later reference.

How to Use:

- **Team Meetings**: Schedule regular video meetings with your team to discuss projects and updates.
- **Webinars**: Host webinars to share knowledge and engage with a larger audience.

Example: Schedule a weekly team meeting to review progress and plan for the upcoming week. Use breakout rooms for smaller group discussions on specific topics.

Conclusion

Leveraging productivity tools and apps can significantly enhance your ability to manage tasks, stay organized, and maintain focus. Tools like Todoist, Trello, and Asana help you organize and prioritize tasks, while time management apps like RescueTime and Forest keep you on track and minimize distractions. Note-taking and knowledge management tools like Evernote, Notion, and OneNote allow you to capture and organize information efficiently. Communication and collaboration tools like Slack, Microsoft Teams, and Zoom facilitate seamless team interactions and project coordination. By integrating these tools into your daily routine, you can boost your productivity and achieve your goals more effectively.

In the next chapter, we will explore how to create a balanced schedule that supports both your professional and personal life, ensuring that you can maintain productivity without sacrificing well-being.

Chapter 8: Creating a Balanced Schedule

Achieving a balanced schedule is essential for maintaining productivity, health, and overall well-being. A well-balanced schedule ensures that you allocate time effectively between work, personal activities, and rest. In this chapter, we will explore strategies for creating a balanced schedule that supports both your professional and personal life.

The Importance of a Balanced Schedule

A balanced schedule allows you to:

1. **Reduce Stress**: Avoid burnout by ensuring you have time for relaxation and hobbies.
2. **Increase Productivity**: Maintain high productivity levels by balancing work with rest and leisure.
3. **Improve Health**: Promote better physical and mental health by scheduling time for exercise, sleep, and self-care.
4. **Enhance Relationships**: Strengthen personal relationships by dedicating time to family and friends.

Steps to Create a Balanced Schedule

1. **Identify Priorities**

Begin by identifying your top priorities in both your professional and personal life. These priorities will guide how you allocate your time.

Steps:

1. **List Your Priorities**: Write down your most important professional and personal goals.
2. **Rank Your Priorities**: Rank them based on importance and urgency.
3. **Allocate Time Accordingly**: Ensure your schedule reflects your top priorities.

Example: If family time is a top priority, allocate specific hours in your schedule for family activities and ensure these are non-negotiable.

2. **Set Boundaries**

Setting boundaries between work and personal life is crucial for maintaining a balanced schedule.

Steps:

1. **Define Work Hours**: Establish clear work hours and stick to them.
2. **Create Personal Time**: Dedicate specific times for personal activities and relaxation.
3. **Communicate Boundaries**: Inform colleagues, clients, and family members of your boundaries.

Example: If you decide to end work by 6 PM, avoid checking work emails or taking work-related calls after this time.

3. **Use a Planner or Calendar**

Using a planner or digital calendar helps you visualize your schedule and ensure you allocate time for all important activities.

Steps:

1. **Choose a Tool**: Select a physical planner or a digital calendar app.
2. **Schedule Everything**: Enter all work tasks, meetings, personal activities, and rest periods into your planner.
3. **Review Regularly**: Review your planner daily to stay on track and make adjustments as needed.

Example: Use Google Calendar to schedule work meetings, gym sessions, family dinners, and personal hobbies. Set reminders to stay on track.

4. **Incorporate Breaks and Downtime**

Scheduling regular breaks and downtime is essential for maintaining productivity and well-being.

Steps:

1. **Plan Short Breaks**: Take short breaks during work hours to rest and recharge.
2. **Schedule Longer Breaks**: Plan longer breaks and leisure activities outside of work hours.
3. **Prioritize Sleep**: Ensure you get adequate sleep by setting a consistent bedtime.

Example: Take a 5-minute break every hour during work and schedule a 30-minute walk or relaxation time after lunch. Ensure you get at least 7-8 hours of sleep each night.

5. **Be Flexible and Adjust**

A balanced schedule requires flexibility to adapt to changing circumstances and unexpected events.

Steps:

1. **Allow Buffer Time**: Include buffer time in your schedule to accommodate unexpected tasks or delays.
2. **Adjust as Needed**: Be prepared to adjust your schedule based on new priorities or changes in your routine.
3. **Reflect and Improve**: Regularly reflect on your schedule and make improvements to maintain balance.

Example: If an urgent work task arises, adjust your schedule to accommodate it but ensure you reschedule your personal time to maintain balance.

6. **Prioritize Self-Care**

Self-care is a crucial component of a balanced schedule. Ensure you dedicate time to activities that promote your physical and mental well-being.

Steps:

1. **Schedule Exercise**: Plan regular exercise sessions to stay healthy.
2. **Practice Mindfulness**: Incorporate mindfulness practices such as meditation or yoga into your routine.
3. **Engage in Hobbies**: Dedicate time to hobbies and activities that bring you joy and relaxation.

Example: Schedule a 30-minute workout every morning and a 10-minute meditation session before bed. Set aside weekends for hobbies like painting or gardening.

7. **Plan for Family and Social Time**

Maintaining strong relationships requires dedicating time to family and social activities.

Steps:

1. **Schedule Family Time**: Plan regular family activities such as dinners, outings, or game nights.
2. **Make Time for Friends**: Schedule regular meetups or calls with friends.
3. **Participate in Community**: Engage in community activities or volunteer work.

Example: Plan a weekly family game night on Fridays and a monthly outing with friends. Volunteer at a local charity once a month.

8. **Review and Reflect**

Regularly reviewing and reflecting on your schedule helps you maintain balance and make necessary adjustments.

Steps:

1. **Weekly Review**: At the end of each week, review your schedule to see what worked and what didn't.
2. **Identify Improvements**: Identify areas where you can improve balance and productivity.

3. **Adjust Accordingly**: Make necessary adjustments to your schedule for the following week.

Example: If you find you're consistently working late, identify why and make changes to delegate tasks or improve time management during work hours.

Practical Tools for Creating a Balanced Schedule

1. **Google Calendar**

Google Calendar is a versatile tool that allows you to schedule and manage both work and personal activities.

Features:

- **Event Scheduling**: Schedule events, set reminders, and invite others.
- **Multiple Calendars**: Create separate calendars for work, personal, and family activities.
- **Integrations**: Integrate with other apps and tools for streamlined scheduling.

How to Use:

- **Plan Your Week**: Schedule all your activities, including work tasks, personal time, and breaks.
- **Set Reminders**: Use reminders to stay on track with your schedule.

Example: Create a work calendar with meetings and deadlines, a personal calendar with exercise and hobbies, and a family calendar with shared activities.

2. **Microsoft Outlook**

Microsoft Outlook is a comprehensive scheduling tool that integrates with email and task management.

Features:

- **Calendar**: Schedule events, set reminders, and share calendars with others.
- **Tasks and To-Do Lists**: Manage tasks and create to-do lists within Outlook.
- **Email Integration**: Integrate calendar events with your email for seamless scheduling.

How to Use:

- **Integrate Work and Personal Schedules**: Use Outlook to manage both your work and personal schedules in one place.
- **Set Priorities**: Prioritize tasks and events to ensure balance.

Example: Use Outlook to schedule work meetings and deadlines, and add personal appointments like doctor visits or social events. Set task priorities to manage your workload.

3. **Trello**

Trello can also be used for personal scheduling and maintaining a balanced life.

Features:

- **Boards and Cards**: Create boards for different aspects of your life and use cards to organize tasks and activities.
- **Labels and Due Dates**: Categorize tasks with labels and set due dates.
- **Checklists**: Use checklists to break down tasks into manageable steps.

How to Use:

- **Personal Planning**: Create a personal planning board with lists for "Work," "Personal," and "Family."
- **Daily and Weekly Planning**: Use Trello to plan your daily and weekly activities.

Example: Create a board with lists for "Work," "Personal," and "Family." Add cards for specific tasks like "Prepare presentation," "Gym session," and "Family dinner," with due dates and checklists.

Maintaining Long-Term Balance

Creating a balanced schedule is an ongoing process that requires regular attention and adjustment. Here are some long-term strategies to maintain balance:

1. **Regular Self-Assessment**

Periodically assess your schedule and overall balance to ensure you are meeting your priorities and maintaining well-being.

Steps:

1. **Monthly Reflection**: Reflect on your schedule and activities at the end of each month.
2. **Adjust Goals**: Adjust your goals and priorities as needed.
3. **Seek Feedback**: Ask for feedback from family, friends, or colleagues on how well you are balancing different aspects of your life.

Example: At the end of each month, review your calendar and assess whether you're spending enough time on personal activities and self-care. Adjust your schedule to better align with your priorities.

2. **Adopt a Growth Mindset**

A growth mindset encourages continuous improvement and adaptability, helping you maintain balance despite changing circumstances.

Steps:

1. **Embrace Challenges**: View challenges as opportunities to learn and grow.
2. **Be Open to Change**: Be willing to adjust your schedule and routines as needed.
3. **Celebrate Progress**: Recognize and celebrate your achievements, no matter how small.

Example: If a new work project demands more of your time, view it as an opportunity to improve time management skills. Adjust your schedule and celebrate small milestones along the way.

3. **Practice Mindfulness**

Mindfulness helps you stay present and focused, reducing stress and enhancing your ability to maintain balance.

Steps:

1. **Daily Practice**: Incorporate mindfulness practices such as meditation or deep breathing into your daily routine.
2. **Mindful Activities**: Engage in activities mindfully, paying full attention to the present moment.
3. **Stress Management**: Use mindfulness techniques to manage stress and stay balanced.

Example: Start your day with a 10-minute meditation session and practice deep breathing during breaks. Approach tasks with full attention and mindfulness.

Conclusion

Creating a balanced schedule is essential for maintaining productivity, health, and overall well-being. By identifying your priorities, setting boundaries, using a planner or calendar, incorporating breaks and downtime, and staying flexible, you can achieve a balanced schedule that supports both your professional and personal life. Regular self-assessment, adopting a growth mindset, and practicing mindfulness further enhance your ability to maintain long-term balance. With a balanced schedule, you can achieve your goals without sacrificing your well-being or personal relationships.

In the next chapter, we will explore the role of habits in time management and how to develop habits that support productivity and balance.

Chapter 9: The Role of Habits in Time Management

Habits play a crucial role in effective time management and productivity. By developing positive habits, you can streamline your daily routines, reduce decision fatigue, and make consistent progress toward your goals. In this chapter, we will explore the importance of habits, how they form, and practical strategies for developing and maintaining habits that support effective time management.

The Importance of Habits

Habits are automatic behaviours that we perform with little conscious thought. Because they require minimal mental effort, habits can help you:

1. **Increase Efficiency**: Automate routine tasks, freeing up mental energy for more complex activities.
2. **Reduce Decision Fatigue**: Minimize the number of decisions you need to make each day, conserving willpower.
3. **Achieve Goals**: Consistently perform actions that contribute to your long-term goals.
4. **Maintain Balance**: Integrate healthy habits into your routine to support well-being and productivity.

How Habits Form

Understanding how habits form can help you develop new ones and change existing ones. Habits are typically formed through a three-step process known as the habit loop:

1. **Cue**: A trigger that initiates the habit. This could be a specific time of day, an emotional state, or an environmental factor.
2. **Routine**: The behaviour or action you perform in response to the cue.
3. **Reward**: The positive outcome or benefit you receive from performing the routine, which reinforces the habit.

Example:

- **Cue**: Your alarm clock rings in the morning.
- **Routine**: You get up and exercise.
- **Reward**: You feel energized and accomplished.

Strategies for Developing Positive Habits

1. **Start Small**

Begin with small, manageable changes that are easy to implement. Small habits are easier to stick to and can be gradually expanded over time.

Steps:

1. **Identify a Small Habit**: Choose a habit that is simple and easy to perform.
2. **Set a Specific Goal**: Define what you want to achieve with the habit.
3. **Build Gradually**: Start with a small version of the habit and gradually increase its complexity or duration.

Example: If you want to start exercising regularly, begin with a 5-minute walk each day. Gradually increase the duration and intensity as the habit becomes established.

2. Use Habit Stacking

Habit stacking involves linking a new habit to an existing one, making it easier to remember and perform.

Steps:

1. **Identify an Existing Habit**: Choose a habit you already perform regularly.
2. **Link the New Habit**: Attach the new habit to the existing one.
3. **Create a Routine**: Develop a routine that incorporates both habits.

Example: If you already brush your teeth every morning, you could add a new habit of doing 10 push-ups immediately afterward.

3. Create a Cue and Reward System

Establish clear cues and rewards to reinforce the new habit and make it more appealing.

Steps:

1. **Define a Cue**: Identify a specific trigger for the habit.
2. **Choose a Reward**: Select a reward that you will receive after performing the habit.
3. **Consistency**: Perform the habit consistently in response to the cue and reward yourself each time.

Example: Set a cue to read a book for 20 minutes each night before bed. Reward yourself with a small treat, like a cup of tea or a piece of chocolate, after reading.

4. Track Your Progress

Tracking your progress helps you stay motivated and see the benefits of the new habit over time.

Steps:

1. **Choose a Tracking Method**: Use a habit tracker app, a journal, or a calendar.
2. **Record Daily**: Mark each day you successfully perform the habit.
3. **Review Regularly**: Review your progress regularly to identify patterns and areas for improvement.

Example: Use a habit tracker app to mark off each day you complete your new habit. Review your progress at the end of each week to stay motivated.

5. Stay Accountable

Accountability can provide motivation and support, helping you stick to your new habits.

Steps:

1. **Find an Accountability Partner**: Choose someone who will support you and hold you accountable.
2. **Set Regular Check-Ins**: Schedule regular check-ins to discuss your progress.
3. **Provide Mutual Support**: Offer support and encouragement to each other.

Example: Partner with a friend to develop a new habit, such as exercising daily. Check in with each other every evening to share your progress and offer support.

6. **Be Patient and Persistent**

Developing new habits takes time and persistence. Be patient with yourself and stay committed to the process.

Steps:

1. **Set Realistic Expectations**: Understand that forming a new habit can take several weeks or months.
2. **Stay Consistent**: Perform the habit consistently, even when it's challenging.
3. **Forgive Setbacks**: If you miss a day, forgive yourself and get back on track the next day.

Example: If you miss a day of your new habit, such as meditation, don't get discouraged. Simply resume your practice the following day and continue moving forward.

Changing Existing Habits

Changing existing habits can be more challenging than forming new ones, but it is possible with the right strategies.

1. **Identify Triggers**

Understand what triggers your existing habit and find ways to disrupt the habit loop.

Steps:

1. **Identify the Cue**: Determine what triggers the habit.
2. **Analyse the Routine**: Understand the behaviour associated with the habit.
3. **Find the Reward**: Identify the reward you receive from the habit.

Example: If you want to stop snacking on junk food in the evening, identify that the cue is watching TV, the routine is eating snacks, and the reward is feeling relaxed.

2. **Replace the Routine**

Replace the unwanted habit with a new, positive routine that provides a similar reward.

Steps:

1. **Choose a Replacement Routine**: Find a new behaviour that can replace the old one.
2. **Maintain the Cue**: Keep the same cue to trigger the new routine.
3. **Ensure a Similar Reward**: Ensure the new routine provides a similar reward.

Example: Replace evening junk food snacking with drinking herbal tea or eating a piece of fruit while watching TV. This keeps the cue and reward similar but changes the routine.

3. **Use Environmental Changes**

Alter your environment to make the unwanted habit more difficult and the desired habit easier.

Steps:

1. **Remove Triggers**: Eliminate triggers for the unwanted habit from your environment.
2. **Add Positive Cues**: Introduce cues that promote the new habit.
3. **Create a Supportive Environment**: Make changes that support the new habit.

Example: Remove junk food from your home and stock healthy snacks. Place a water bottle on your desk to remind you to stay hydrated.

4. **Seek Support**

Enlist the help of friends, family, or a support group to help you change the habit.

Steps:

1. **Communicate Your Goals**: Let others know about your goal to change the habit.
2. **Ask for Support**: Ask for their support and encouragement.
3. **Join a Group**: Consider joining a support group for additional motivation and accountability.

Example: If you're trying to quit smoking, tell your friends and family about your goal and ask for their support. Join a smoking cessation group for additional resources and encouragement.

5. **Practice Self-Compassion**

Be kind to yourself throughout the process of changing habits. Recognize that setbacks are a normal part of the journey.

Steps:

1. **Acknowledge Challenges**: Accept that changing habits can be difficult.
2. **Practice Self-Forgiveness**: Forgive yourself for any setbacks and focus on moving forward.
3. **Celebrate Progress**: Celebrate small victories and progress along the way.

Example: If you have a setback, such as skipping a workout, acknowledge the challenge and forgive yourself. Celebrate your overall progress and keep moving forward.

Building a Routine Around Positive Habits

1. **Morning Routine**

Start your day with a morning routine that sets a positive tone and prepares you for a productive day.

Steps:

1. **Wake Up Early**: Wake up at a consistent time each morning.
2. **Exercise**: Incorporate physical activity to boost energy levels.
3. **Plan Your Day**: Review your schedule and set your intentions for the day.
4. **Mindfulness**: Practice mindfulness or meditation to start the day with a clear mind.

Example: Wake up at 6 AM, go for a 30-minute jog, review your daily planner, and spend 10 minutes meditating before starting work.

2. **Workday Routine**

Develop a workday routine that promotes focus, productivity, and balance.

Steps:

1. **Time Blocking**: Use time blocking to allocate specific periods for different tasks.
2. **Breaks**: Schedule regular breaks to rest and recharge.
3. **Prioritize Tasks**: Start with the most important tasks first.
4. **Limit Distractions**: Create a work environment that minimizes distractions.

Example: Block out 9-11 AM for focused work, take a 10-minute break, then continue with administrative tasks until lunch. Avoid checking emails during focused work periods.

3. **Evening Routine**

End your day with an evening routine that helps you unwind and prepare for the next day.

Steps:

1. **Reflect on the Day**: Review what you accomplished and what needs to be carried over.
2. **Plan for Tomorrow**: Prepare a to-do list for the next day.
3. **Relax**: Engage in relaxing activities such as reading or listening to music.

4. **Sleep Hygiene**: Follow a consistent bedtime routine to ensure quality sleep.

Example: Spend 10 minutes reviewing your day, create a to-do list for tomorrow, read a book for 20 minutes, and go to bed at the same time each night.

Conclusion

Habits play a vital role in effective time management and productivity. By understanding how habits form and using strategies such as starting small, habit stacking, and creating a cue and reward system, you can develop positive habits that support your goals. Changing existing habits involves identifying triggers, replacing routines, and seeking support. Building routines around positive habits in your morning, workday, and evening can further enhance your productivity and balance. With patience, persistence, and self-compassion, you can create lasting habits that contribute to a more productive and fulfilling life.

In the next chapter, we will summarize the key points covered in this book and provide a comprehensive guide to mastering your time and achieving your goals.

Chapter 10: Your Path to Mastery: A Comprehensive Guide

Congratulations on making it to the final chapter! By now, you have learned various strategies and techniques to manage your time effectively, set and achieve goals, overcome procrastination, and develop positive habits. In this chapter, we will summarize the key points covered in this book and provide a comprehensive guide to mastering your time and achieving your goals.

Recap of Key Concepts

1. **The Importance of Time Management**
   - Time is a finite and irreplaceable resource.
   - Effective time management increases productivity, reduces stress, and improves work-life balance.
2. **Setting SMART Goals**
   - Specific, Measurable, Achievable, Relevant, and Time-bound (SMART) goals provide clear direction and motivation.
   - Break larger goals into smaller, manageable tasks.
3. **Prioritizing Tasks Effectively**
   - Techniques like the Eisenhower Matrix, ABCDE Method, and Pareto Principle help prioritize tasks based on their importance and urgency.
   - Focus on high-priority tasks to maximize productivity.
4. **Techniques for Better Time Management**
   - The Pomodoro Technique, time blocking, the 2-Minute Rule, and batch processing enhance focus and efficiency.

- Use mind mapping and time management apps to stay organized.
5. **Overcoming Procrastination**
    - Understand the psychological factors behind procrastination and use strategies like breaking tasks into smaller steps and the 5-Minute Rule.
    - Create a productive environment and seek accountability.
6. **Tools and Apps to Boost Productivity**
    - Task management tools (Todoist, Trello, Asana), time management apps (RescueTime, Forest, Pomodone), and note-taking tools (Evernote, Notion, OneNote) enhance organization and focus.
    - Communication and collaboration tools (Slack, Microsoft Teams, Zoom) facilitate teamwork.
7. **Creating a Balanced Schedule**
    - Identify priorities, set boundaries, use a planner or calendar, and incorporate breaks and downtime.
    - Regularly review and adjust your schedule to maintain balance.
8. **The Role of Habits in Time Management**
    - Develop positive habits using strategies like starting small, habit stacking, and creating a cue and reward system.
    - Change existing habits by identifying triggers and replacing routines.

Comprehensive Guide to Mastering Your Time

Now, let's integrate these concepts into a comprehensive guide that you can follow to master your time and achieve your goals.

1. **Assess Your Current Situation**

Steps:

- Conduct a time audit to understand how you currently spend your time.
- Identify areas where you can improve and eliminate time-wasting activities.

Example: Track your daily activities for a week using a time-tracking app like RescueTime. Analyse the data to identify patterns and areas for improvement.

2. **Set Clear Goals**

Steps:

- Define your short-term and long-term goals using the SMART criteria.
- Break down larger goals into smaller, actionable tasks.

Example: Set a SMART goal to "complete a professional certification within six months" and break it down into tasks like "research programs," "enrol in a course," and "study for one hour daily."

3. **Prioritize Tasks**

Steps:

- Use the Eisenhower Matrix to categorize tasks based on urgency and importance.
- Focus on high-priority tasks and delegate or eliminate low-priority ones.

Example: Create a daily to-do list and categorize tasks using the Eisenhower Matrix. Prioritize tasks in the "Urgent and Important" quadrant.

4. **Plan and Schedule**

   Steps:

   - Use a planner or digital calendar to schedule tasks, meetings, and personal activities.
   - Incorporate time management techniques like the Pomodoro Technique and time blocking.

   Example: Use Google Calendar to schedule focused work blocks, breaks, and personal activities. Implement the Pomodoro Technique for tasks requiring intense focus.

5. **Develop Positive Habits**

   Steps:

   - Start with small, manageable habits and gradually build on them.
   - Use habit stacking to link new habits to existing ones.

   Example: Start a habit of daily exercise by adding a 5-minute walk after your morning coffee. Gradually increase the duration and intensity of the exercise.

6. **Overcome Procrastination**

   Steps:

- Identify triggers for procrastination and implement strategies to address them.
- Use techniques like the 5-Minute Rule and accountability partners to stay on track.

Example: If you tend to procrastinate on starting large projects, break them down into smaller tasks and commit to working on the first task for just five minutes.

7. **Utilize Productivity Tools**

   Steps:

   - Choose and integrate task management, time management, and note-taking tools into your workflow.
   - Use communication and collaboration tools to enhance teamwork and coordination.

   Example: Use Trello to manage projects, RescueTime to track productivity, and Slack for team communication.

8. **Maintain a Balanced Schedule**

   Steps:

   - Regularly review and adjust your schedule to ensure balance between work, personal activities, and rest.
   - Set boundaries and prioritize self-care to prevent burnout.

Example: Schedule weekly reviews of your calendar to ensure you are maintaining a balance between work commitments and personal activities.

9. **Reflect and Improve**

   Steps:

   - Regularly reflect on your progress and identify areas for improvement.
   - Adjust your strategies and habits as needed to stay on track.

   Example: Spend 10 minutes each evening reflecting on your day. Identify what went well and what could be improved, and adjust your plan for the next day accordingly.

Action Plan for Mastering Your Time

To put this comprehensive guide into practice, here is an actionable plan:

1. **Week 1: Conduct a Time Audit**
   - Track your activities and analyse how you spend your time.
   - Identify time-wasting activities and areas for improvement.
2. **Week 2: Set Goals and Prioritize Tasks**
   - Define your SMART goals and break them down into actionable tasks.
   - Use the Eisenhower Matrix to prioritize tasks.
3. **Week 3: Plan and Schedule**

- Use a planner or digital calendar to schedule your tasks and activities.
- Implement the Pomodoro Technique and time blocking.
4. **Week 4: Develop Positive Habits**
    - Start small with new habits and use habit stacking.
    - Track your habits and review your progress.
5. **Week 5: Overcome Procrastination**
    - Identify procrastination triggers and implement strategies to address them.
    - Use the 5-Minute Rule and seek accountability.
6. **Week 6: Utilize Productivity Tools**
    - Choose and integrate task management, time management, and note-taking tools.
    - Enhance teamwork with communication and collaboration tools.
7. **Week 7: Maintain a Balanced Schedule**
    - Regularly review and adjust your schedule for balance.
    - Prioritize self-care and set boundaries.
8. **Ongoing: Reflect and Improve**
    - Reflect on your progress regularly and make necessary adjustments.
    - Stay committed to continuous improvement and adaptability.

Conclusion

Mastering your time is a journey that requires dedication, self-awareness, and continuous effort. By applying the strategies and techniques outlined in this book, you can take control of your time, achieve your goals, and lead a more productive and fulfilling life. Remember that the key to success lies in consistent practice, flexibility, and a willingness to learn and adapt. Stay committed to your path of mastery, and you will reap the rewards of effective time management and a balanced life.

Thank you for embarking on this journey with me. Here's to your success in mastering your time and achieving your dreams!

Closing Remarks

Thank you for embarking on this journey toward mastering your time and boosting your productivity. I hope that the strategies and insights shared in this book have provided you with valuable tools and practical steps to take control of your schedule and achieve your goals.

Remember, time management is not a one-size-fits-all solution. It's about finding what works best for you and continually refining your approach. Stay patient, be kind to yourself, and celebrate your progress along the way.

As you move forward, keep in mind that the key to effective time management is intentionality. Focus on what truly matters, make conscious choices, and prioritize your well-being. By doing so, you can create a balanced, fulfilling life that aligns with your personal and professional aspirations.

Thank you for allowing me to be a part of your journey. Here's to your success in mastering your time and achieving your dreams. Every moment counts, so make the most of each one.

www.ingramcontent.com/pod-product-compliance
Lightning Source LLC
Chambersburg PA
CBHW072052230526
45479CB00010B/847